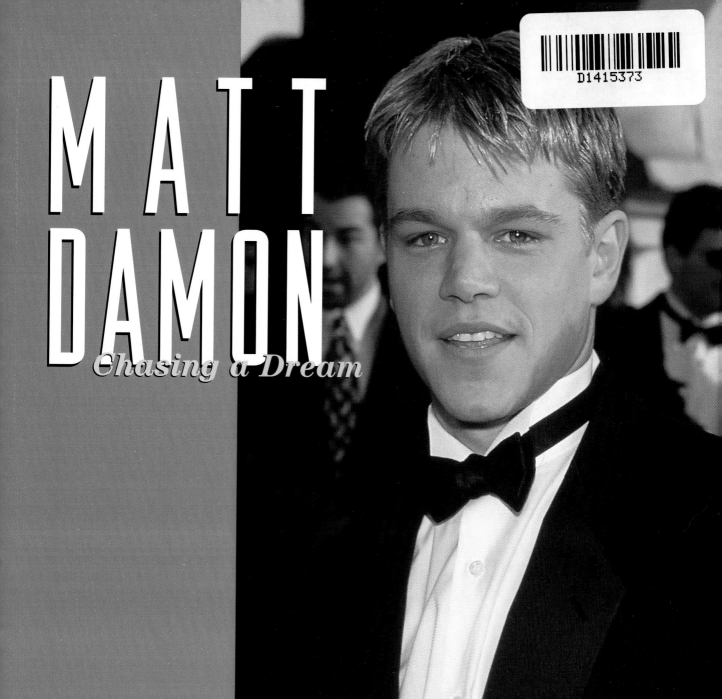

MATT DAMON

Chasing a Dream

D1415373

MATT DAMON

Chasing a Dream

BY MARK BEGO

A JOHN BOSWELL ASSOCIATES BOOK

**Andrews McMeel
Publishing**

Kansas City

Matt Damon: Chasing a Dream copyright © 1998 by John Boswell Management, Inc. All rights reserved. Printed in the U.S.A. No part of this book may be used or reproduced in any manner whatsoever without written permission except in the case of reprints in the context of reviews. For information, write Andrews McMeel Publishing, an Andrews McMeel Universal company, 4520 Main Street, Kansas City, Missouri 64111.

www.andrewsmcmeel.com

Library of Congress Cataloging-in-Publication Data on file
ISBN: 0-8362-7131-9

Cover and book design by Charles Kreloff

ATTENTION SCHOOLS AND BUSINESSES
Andrews McMeel books are available at quantity discounts with bulk purchase for educational, business, or sales promotional use. For information, please write to: Special Sales Department, Andrews McMeel Publishing, 4520 Main Street, Kansas City, Missouri 64111.

DEDICATION

To Marie Morreale: You are one of the most generous and giving friends I have ever met. Thanks for passing *Leonardo DiCaprio: Romantic Hero* on to me, and for always being a guardian angel.

ACKNOWLEDGMENTS

Robert Bennett
Eden Blackwood
John Boswell and Patty Brown
Trippy Cunningham
William Dawson
R. Couri Hay
Glenn Hughes
Isiah James
Christine Jampolsky
Charles Kreloff
Sindi Markoff Kaplan
Ruffa & Ruffa
Peter Schekeryk and Melanie
Jim Thompson and Melitta Coffee
Stanley Turer
Mary Wilson

PHOTO CREDITS

Pages 1,36 & 71 Fitzroy Barrett/Globe Photos, Inc; Pages 9 & 36 Lisa Rose/Globe Photos, Inc.; Pages 8,10,12,45,46,47,48,51, 55,60 & 65 Globe Photos, Inc.; Pages 18,21 & 78 Sonia Moskowitz/Globe Photos, Inc; Page 38 Rangefinders/Globe Photos, Inc.; Front Cover and Pages 39,81,85,86 & 89 Henry McGee/Globe Photos, Inc.; Page 77 Steve Finn/Globe Photos, Inc.; Pages 82 & 83 Laura Cavanaugh/Globe Photos, Inc; Page 70 Roger Harvey/Globe Photos, Inc; Page 5 Jerry Lowe/SAGA/Archive Photos; Back Cover and Page 29 Miles Aranowitz/ Archive Photos; Pages 30 & 44 Fotos International/Archive Photos: Page 32 John Seaward/Archive Photos; Pages 73 & 75 Reuters/Sam Mircovich/Archive Photos; Page 74 Reuters/Gary Hershorn/Archive Photos; Page 72 Reuters/Fred Prouser/ Archive Photos; Back Cover and Page 79 Kosta Alexander/Fotos International/ Archive Photos; Back Cover and Pages 6,11,19 Vincent Zuffante/Star File Photo; Pages 15, 22 Pen Zuffante/Star File Photo; Pages 13,16,17,37 & 96, Jeffrey Mayer/Star File Photo; Page 90 Star File Photo; all other photographs courtesy of Photofest.

Contents

Writer, Actor, Boy Wonder

He's 27 years old, and has a smile that exudes youthful enthusiasm and charm. He is talented, confident, personable, and totally dedicated to his craft. He is also focused, determined, and one of the hottest and most sought-after young men in Hollywood today. In the span of one year, Matt Damon has watched his movie career elevate from the status of mere footnote to that of history-making major-league film stardom. Thanks to the inspirational and deeply emotional screenplay that he penned with his best friend, Ben Affleck, and an acting performance that brilliantly lit up the screen, he has taken *Good Will Hunting* from a roughly written project and watched it blossom

Matt Damon's career virtually exploded in 1998.

Showering off in *School Ties*.

With Danny DeVito in *The Rainmaker*.

that they wanted to become actors when they grew up. Who would have thought that the duo's pipe dreams would grow into such a victorious tale of achievement? Not since the days of young Orson Wells and his *Citizen Kane* has there been such a youthful Best Screenplay Oscar-winning triumph in Tinsel Town. In addition to the Academy Award, their screenplay also won a Golden Globe Award and the National Board of Review's "Special Achievement in Filmmaking" Award, in addition to landing on several of 1997's most prestigious year-end "Top Ten" movie review lists.

Matt never graduated from college, but instead dropped out of Harvard a year shy of attaining his degree. He packed himself up for Hollywood, where he joined Ben, lived on the sofas of friends, and existed on Spam sandwiches and beer. Damon landed supporting roles in a string of films, including 1988's *Mystic Pizza* and *School Ties*, and TV films, including *Rising Son*, *The Good Old Boys,* and *Geronimo: An American Legend*. He also went to a slew of auditions, trying out for several film roles, including the part of "The Kid" that Leonardo DiCaprio landed in Sharon Stone's *The Quick and the Dead*, and the

into one of the major Hollywood success stories of the decade.

A pair of twenty-something wannabe actors from Boston, Matt and Ben spent their childhood as close buddies with big dreams. Although their parents tried to talk them out of it, they both insisted

plum role of Robin in the big-budget extravaganza *Batman Forever*. Meanwhile, Ben landed one of the starring roles in the cult film *Chasing Amy*, and Matt was seen for a few seconds in the same movie in a cameo role.

Matt's one shot at big-time stardom came in Francis Ford Coppola's screen adaptation of John Grisham's *The Rainmaker*. While Damon received glowing reviews, the film found him cast as the lead character in an ensemble cast of established stars, including Danny DeVito, John Voight, Roy Scheider, Mickey Rourke, Theresa Wright, and Mary Kay Place. Although he was in great company, and turned in an appealingly believable characterization, it was not to become a star-making turn for him.

In the mid-1990s, as they both found themselves moving very slowly up the show-business food chain, neither Damon nor Affleck seemed to find the kind of roles that set them apart from the pack. Instead of leaving their futures in the hands of agents and the luck of the draw, they decided to take one of Matt's old college writing projects and turn it into the kind of feature film they could both really sink their teeth into. This is how the screenplay for *Good Will Hunting* began to take

Matt Damon, Minnie Driver, and Ben Affleck at the premiere of *Good Will Hunting*.

shape. Naturally, it was not a matter of "overnight success." Matt recalls, "It was five years of our lives. Ben and I put everything we had in it."

Much to the surprise of everyone, they not only managed to sell the screenplay, but also insisted on starring in the film as well. On the night of March 23, 1998, Matt Damon and Ben Affleck received

the kind of diploma that no college could give them: an Academy Award for Best Original Screenplay.

As they stood on the stage of the Shrine Auditorium in Los Angeles amidst the live, internationally viewed telecast, each clutching their Oscars, it was an incredibly exciting sight to watch. Their moment of glory was even more magnified by the fact that

"I've gone from eating fried ramen noodles out of the box to eating real spaghetti."

they had been presented their trophies by another legendary Hollywood team, Jack Lemmon and Walter Matthau. One couldn't help but wonder whether or not Damon and Affleck will forever be linked in their careers in the same way that Lemmon and Matthau are.

Along with their own victorious win for Best Original Screenplay, Damon and Affleck's script brought Oscar glory to three-time-nominated Robin Williams, in the category of Best Supporting Actor, for playing Damon's therapist in *Good Will Hunting*. All in all, the film garnered nine separate nominations, including Best Picture, and a Best Actress nomination for Damon's leading lady, Minnie Driver.

According to Matt, "For as long as I can remember, I've wanted to be an actor." But he could only have dreamed of the kind of success he has experienced because of *Good Will Hunting*.

Everyone associated with *Good Will Hunting* has nothing but glowing things to say about him. Among his biggest fans is Robin Williams, who attests, "[Matt is an] amazing talent, and he's a gentle, good person." And the film's director, Gus Van Sant emphasizes his bright future in the film busi-

Minnie and Matt not only heated up the screen together, but shared an off-screen romance as well.

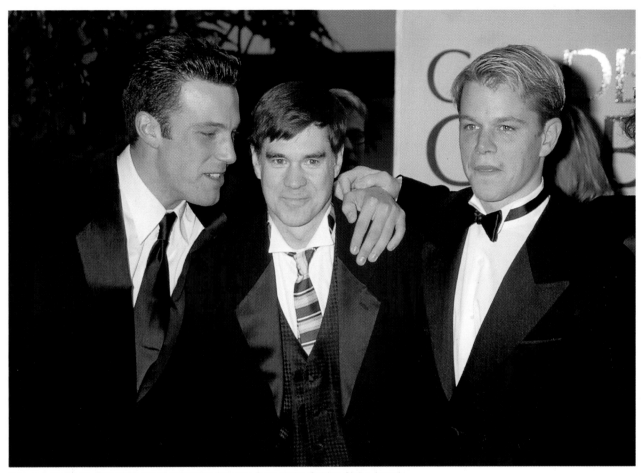

Ben and Matt with *Good Will Hunting* director Gus Van Sant at the Golden Globe Awards.

ness by explaining, "Matt has a great face. So, that's always great. But what makes him appealing is he's bringing a character to life so specifically that it's mesmerizing."

Since winning the Oscars, both Matt and Ben have become two of the hottest properties in Hollywood. Matt's list of current and forthcoming projects includes *Saving Private Ryan* with Tom Hanks; *Dogma* with Ben Affleck, Emma Thompson, Alan Rickman, and Linda Fiorentino; *The Talented Mr. Ripley*, which is being directed by Anthony Minghella, whose last film was *The English Patient*; *Rounders* with John Malkovich, Ed Norton, John Turturro, and Martin Landau; as well as lending his voice to the animated film *Planet Ice*.

"I've gone from eating fried ramen noodles out of the box to eating real spaghetti," Damon laughs. In fact, he is so amazed at the 180-degree turn that his career has taken, he proclaims, "It's like I'm living somebody else's life."

Although Matt's and Ben's

careers have gone through the stratosphere, they both claim that they are as grounded as they were before Oscar smiled upon them. Far from having gone on a Hollywood ego trip, Matt explains, "We're constantly accused by people who come in and out of our circle of friends that we're the most boring people ever. There are people who go, 'I got tickets to see so-and-so, and why don't you guys come?' We're like, 'Yeah, whatever,' and end up at the same bar every night with the same people telling the same old jokes. We've always been that way."

Some things have changed, however. Neither Matt nor Ben can just go and hang out on Sunset Boulevard and roam unrecognized into Starbuck's, or Tower Records, or Ralph's grocery store like they did before. They are both known by virtually everyone under the sun as two of today's hottest "sex symbols." Instead of letting this go to their heads, they remain more perplexed by this phenomenon than the rest of the world. "That part is

Van Sant coaches Minnie and Matt between scenes of *Good Will Hunting*.

really weird," Damon claims. "I live kind of a very monkish life."

As Hollywood's most unconventional "sex symbol," Matt's personal and creative life still poses several fascinating questions. Among them: What is his friendship with Ben really like? Are they as close as ever, or are they now rivals? What are the parallels between the real-life Damon and Affleck, and the characters they portray in *Good Will Hunting*? How does Matt feel about portraying the lead role in *Good Will Hunting*, while Ben's role was a supporting one? Are Matt and Ben planning on centering their attention on their acting, or are they continuing their screenplay writing careers? What is the truth about Matt's affair with Minnie Driver? What went wrong, and are they still friends? And, where does he see his career heading in the future?

"I don't want to be a flash in the pan," he proclaims. "I don't want to lose it all." Far from that. It is clear that Matt Damon's career is just beginning, and there are very big things looming on his horizon. He has paid his dues for several years to arrive at the enviable position in which he now finds himself within the show business realm. And, this is his story.

Ben and Matt score at the Golden Globe Awards, January 18, 1998.

A Creative Childhood

Matt Damon was born on October 8, 1970, the younger child in a family of two boys. Their mother, Nancy Carlsson-Paige, is a noted child-development expert who teaches early childhood education at Lesley College in Cambridge, Massachusetts. Their father, Kent Damon, is a Boston-area tax accountant. Both Matt and his brother, Kyle, were encouraged from an early age to

Matt as a boy gone bad.

become creative and imaginative. While Matt gravitated towards acting, his older brother, Kyle, has become an artist, specializing in sculpture.

Their parents divorced when Matt was only two years old, but he has remained close to both of his parents. An adventurous, new-age kind of gal, Matt's mom moved herself and her two boys into an experimental co-op house in Boston, where they lived together in a kind of post-hippie commune atmosphere. According to Matt, "About six families bought a broken-down house in Central Square and rebuilt it. It was governed by a shared philosophy that housing is a basic human right. Every week there was the three-hour community meeting, and Sundays were workdays. My mom put little masks on me and my brother, gave us goggles and crowbars, and we demo'd [demolished] the walls."

At the age of nine, Matt appeared on a local children's television show, and once he found himself in front of the cameras, that was it, he wanted to become an actor. Not long afterward he met his lifelong buddy, Ben Affleck. "We were basically best friends since I was ten and he was

Matt with his father and mother, attending the 1998 *Vanity Fair* Oscar party at Morton's in Beverly Hills.

Ben and Matt have both maintained strong relationships with their mothers, who were their dates at the Academy Awards.

eight," Matt recalls.

The connection was originally made through their mothers. "My mother is the professor of early childhood development, and she knew of Ben's mother—who's a teacher of little kids—and sought her out after we moved back to Cambridge. So I was pretty much

forced into hanging out with Ben," he laughs.

Matt's mom absolutely forbid her boys to have toy guns, or any toys that in any way promoted violence. According to him, "My mother had written some books on war play and those cartoons that are like commercials for action fig-

ures. What worried my mother about those shows was not only that they encouraged violent play, but also that they hampered creativity. So growing up for me was like you'd get some blocks and then you'd have to go make up a game. I was always making up stories and acting out plays; that's just the way I was raised. Ben came from a more prestigious acting background."

Whenever the two of them are in the same room, they still banter back and forth about their childhood together. "I remember exactly what he was like: gregarious, outgoing," says Matt of Ben. "It was no surprise that he grew up into the totally obnoxious guy he is now," he laughs. "Number one, he claims that I never struck him out in Little League [baseball]. Which is total bulls***—I was the best pitcher in the league."

According to Matt, he was always very outgoing, and loved sports. For a long time he was obsessed with becoming a basketball player, until one day his father gave him a bit of a "reality check." As he explains it, "I knew since I was twelve that I was going to be an actor. I was originally going to be a basketball player. Tiny Archibald was my favorite player—he's called Tiny because he's only six foot one [inch tall]. My father sat me down and said, 'I'm the tallest Damon ever to evolve and I'm five [foot] eleven [inches tall]. But I'm never going to play in the NBA.' I gave up basketball at that moment and took up acting. Whatever I did, I wanted to be the best at it.

Matt and Ben have been best friends since they were ages ten and eight, respectively.

Matt and Ben at *The National Board of Review* party at New York City's famed Tavern on the Green restaurant.

I remember that moment in *The Natural* when Robert Redford says, 'I just want to walk down the street and have people say, "There goes Roy Hobbs, the best there ever was."'"

Matt's father also brought his boys up to be creative from an early age. "[He] encouraged my brother and me to be imaginative. I took classes. I was in a kabuki play when I was 13," he says.

Kyle Damon recalls, "We didn't rebel much. We didn't do drugs, stay out late or bad-mouth our parents."

Almost immediately, Kyle began showing off his creative side. He would make costumes out of paper and cardboard, and Matt and Ben and he would act out scenes from movies they had seen.

That gave way to the notion that Ben and Matt should grow up to become actors. At the age of 12, Matt started doing theater in school, and taking pantomime classes. Says Matt, "Every time we sat down to dinner, Chris [Ben Affleck's mom] would say, 'Why don't you guys become doctors?'"

She may as well have just gone all out and suggested that they become brain surgeons. Once Matt and Ben were fixated on acting, there was no deterring them.

Matt always seemed to know that
he was destined to be a star.

Two Buddies From Boston

	MATT DAMON	BEN AFFLECK
BIRTHDATE:	October 8, 1970	August 15, 1972
ASTROLOGICAL SIGN:	Libra	Leo
BIRTHSTONE:	Sapphire	Peridot
AGE AT THE TIME OF ACADEMY AWARD TELECAST:	27	25
UNFORGETTABLE ROLE IN A SCHOOL PLAY:	A sex-starved Greek soldier in *Lysistrata*	Hookah-smoking caterpillar in *Alice in Wonderland*
GOOD WILL HUNTING CHARACTER NAME:	Will	Chucki
PERSONAL IMAGE:	All-American Preppy	Blue-Collar Hot
PEOPLE FROM HISTORY THEY WISH THEY COULD MEET:	William Shakespeare Alexander the Great Napoleon	Teddy Roosevelt
LENGTHS TO WHICH THEY WILL GO FOR THE IDEAL MOVIE ROLE:	Starved himself into losing 40 pounds for his part in *Courage Under Fire*	Once lost a movie role for not being able to cry on cue, so he spent a year practicing his tear skills
MOST FAMOUS LOVE AFFAIR:	Minnie Driver	Gwyneth Paltrow
NOTABLE EARLY FILM ROLE:	*Mystic Pizza*	*Dazed & Confused*
STAR-MAKING MOVIE:	*The Rainmaker*	*Chasing Amy*

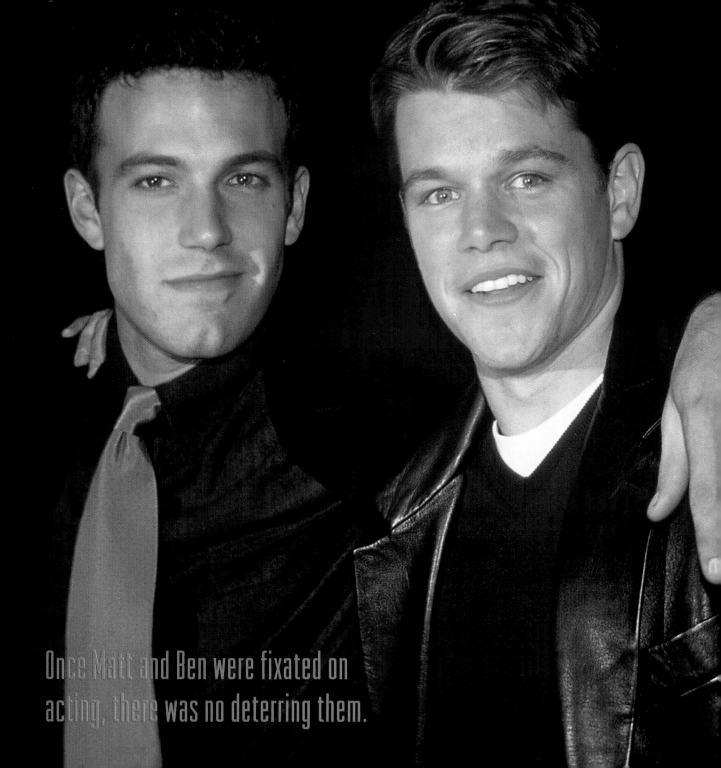

Once Matt and Ben were fixated on acting, there was no deterring them.

Educating Matt

With the goal of pursuing an acting career firmly in their minds, Matt and his best buddy began seeking out every class, and every theatrical production they could find. High school classes and plays became a firm groundwork for their aspirations.

Damon recalls, "I had an amazing drama teacher in high school named Gerry Speca, and Ben and I owe everything to him."

Speca today looks up to Matt as his star pupil. According to him, "He was this little dervish, running around, rehearsing his part, all his moves, making sure everything was just right. [*Rainmaker* co-star] Mary Kay Place has talked about how generous he is, how hard he works, and all those qualities were in evidence when he was a kid."

He and Ben used to get together every

Matt in *Geronimo:
An American Legend.*

At the age of nine, Matt appeared on a local children's television show, and once he found himself in front of the cameras, that was it— he wanted to become an actor.

chance they had to plot out their creative futures. "We used to have what we called 'business lunches' in high school, which meant we met at the smaller cafeteria and got a table," he recalls.

Although Matt's mother had encouraged both of her sons to become creative and imaginative, she was appalled to find that her youngest son had a larger than average ego attached to his aspirations. "I was talking to my mother one day," he says, "this was when I was sixteen or seventeen—and she goes, 'Matt, why are you so obsessed with acting?' And I said, 'Because someday I want to walk down the street and have people say, "There goes Matt Damon, the best there ever was."' And she said, 'Did I raise you? That's just an egomaniacal pipe dream. How does it help other people?' Of course I hadn't given much thought to that."

Being an "actor" and being a "star" are terms all too often confused for each other. Everyone wants to grow up to be a star in whichever field of endeavor they pursue; however, there also has to be a love for the craft as well. Along the way, Matt developed a love of acting as well as a desire for the fame and notoriety that can go along with it.

Speaking of his hometown, Matt fondly looks back and jokes, "Cambridge is not that big a town. It's like the People's Republic of Cambridge."

Ben Affleck's younger brother Casey laughingly says of Matt, "He was the guy who sat in the back of the [school] bus always making out with his girlfriends."

He is also fondly remembered back there as well. His teachers at Cambridge Rindge and Latin, the public high school he attended, are glowingly proud of him and his accomplishments in Hollywood. Social studies teacher Larry Anderson claims, "I knew some day the magazines would be calling. Matt can act. He can sing. He can dance. And, he's good-looking. When I watched *Good Will Hunting* at a screening, sitting between him and Ben, with each like I would grab them and kiss them. They were perfect."

At first, Matt thought about

Matt, in the background, co-starred with Brian Dennehy in 1990's *Rising Son*.

Damon with Jason Patric in *Geronimo: An American Legend*.

blowing off his senior year in high school all together, running away to the Big Apple, and concentrating on the task of being a struggling actor in Manhattan. "At 16 I said, 'I'm ready. I'm going pro,'" he explains. "I went to New York with some money I'd made doing a commercial and got an agent. He turned out to be a bad agent, which was good for me, because I didn't get any work, so I went back and did well in school."

In 1988, at the age of 17, he landed his first movie role. It was an experience that really cemented his desire to become a full-time professional film actor, as opposed to a commercial or stage actor. Although his movie role was a mere one-line bit that you have to pay attention to the screen to find, through the experience he really caught the acting bug. An amusing film about a circle of friends who work at a pizza parlor in an ocean-side town, *Mystic Pizza* is most noted for turning one of its stars into an international sensation: Julia Roberts. For Matt, stardom was still several years away.

As his graduation from high school loomed in the future, he had begun applying to colleges. His first choice was Harvard. Looking back on this era he says, "They saw that I was dedicated to something and that I tried hard at it. The opening line in the essay for my application to Harvard was, 'For as long as I can remember, I've wanted to be an actor.'"

Much to his thrill, he was indeed accepted at Harvard, and off he went to college. However,

Terry Kinney, Matt Damon, Blayne Weaver, Tommy Lee Jones, and Sam Shepard in *The Good Old Boys*.

had the right opportunity come along sooner, he would have gladly put college on "hold" indefinitely. Matt recalls, "My freshman year I got a call to meet the head of Touchstone Pictures in New York. And it turns out to be an audition for *The Mickey Mouse Club* on the Disney Channel, with [mouse] ears and everything. Then I had to go back to school and everyone was asking me how the audition went." As it turned out, Damon was not destined to become a mouse-eared TV star.

At Harvard, his acting classes were what he was the most

excited about. Instructor David Wheeler still speaks of Damon's powerful characterization during a scene from Sam Shephard's *Fool for Love*. Attests Wheeler, "It was extremely mature and powerful and a total surprise. What was immediately clear was that he was very, very talented. I think he's right up there with the best actors I've worked with. Absolutely. They're all different, of course. But what Matt has shown steadily is the courage to be himself." (Who could have known at the time, that in 1995 Matt would be co-starring in the made-for-TV

movie *Good Old Boys* with none other than actor/playwright Shephard himself?)

Matt was so determined to attain some notoriety as an actor that he was clearly on the right path. He was getting his education, he had strong will and determination; all he would need to become a success were the right breaks. There was clearly no stopping him from chasing his dream.

Matt, Tommy Lee, and Blayne on horseback in *The Good Old Boys*.

Chasing A Dream

Matt in *School Ties* in 1992.

While he excelled in acting and theater classes, he did less well in his other studies. English was a subject that fell into the later category. When opportunities for outside acting assignments came along, his homework ran a distant second on his list of priorities. It wasn't long before Matt was to realize that he was getting a better education on the sets of film and TV movies than he was getting out of the classrooms and textbooks. It was inevitable that eventually he would reach an impasse and have to make a decision.

"It was just so exciting to get into Harvard. But I didn't do so well when I got there," Matt admits. "I screwed up and got the gentleman's B minus, which is basically what they give you when you really should

School Ties stars Brendan Fraser, Randall Batinkoff, Andrew Lowery, Anthony Rapp, Chris O'Donnell, Ben Affleck, Cole Hauser, and Matt Damon.

be flunking. They'd don't like to acknowledge that they admitted the wrong person. I was 17, just going out and having a good time, playing pool. After my first year, I did [the TV movie] *Rising Son* and then when I went back to school, I really dug it. Where else can you relax and study Japanese culture?"

Meanwhile, Matt's best friend, Ben, graduated from high school, packed up his bags and headed out to Hollywood to try to get himself into the movies. Although they were now on separate coasts, they remained in constant contact.

It was during this same era that the beginnings of the script that would eventually become *Good Will Hunting* was born. "I was doing a playwriting class and a theater directing class with David Wheeler, who knew this world that Ben and I both came from," says Damon. "And when Ben came back from L.A. for Christmas, I showed him this thing I'd written and—because he knows David, too—he came into the class and we acted it out. It was a scene from what later became *Good Will Hunting*. Then, when spring break came around the following March, I went to L.A. to audition for a part in *Geronimo*, which I ended up getting. By then I had this forty-page thing and didn't know what to do with it. I gave it to Ben, and he looked at it and said, 'This is really good. We should write this together.' And I said, 'I know, but I don't know where it should go,' and he said, 'I don't either,' but we agreed to write it." However, after Christmas break, the script was put on the shelf, where it was to remain for the time being.

Between attending Harvard and taking time off to appear in films, Matt Damon was getting a great education. At Harvard he was learning about the mechanics of acting and screenplay writing, and on the movie sets he was learning firsthand how a movie was actually produced. "I left again to do *School Ties* and *Geronimo*, and then I went back for a third year," he explains.

Filming *Geronimo: An American Legend* was an especially exciting experience for Matt. Not only did he get to work alongside an Academy Award–winning actor, Robert Duvall, but he also had the chance to spend some time on horseback on location in Moab, Utah. In the film, Matt portrayed the role of real-life historical figure 2nd Lt. Britton Davis, a U.S. Cavalry Officer who was assigned the

"At 16 I said, 'I'm ready. I'm going pro,'" he explains. "I went to New York with some money I'd made doing a commercial and got an agent."

dangerous mission of capturing famed Apache Chief Geronimo. "I was taught to observe real people, to study from life, by Robert Duvall when we did *Geronimo*," Matt recalls. "It was really awesome to play a character who wrote an autobiography. I read it, like, 20 times."

Although the acting assignment sounds like a potential vacation at a dude ranch for Damon, getting up at 5:00 A.M. every day, and sitting on the back of a horse for 12 hours a day got a little old after a while. "It was fun," he admits, "but by the end, everybody was ready to get the hell out of there."

It turned out to be a great acting experience for Damon to appear in such a prestigious television movie with Jason Patric and Robert Duvall. However, it would have been beyond his wildest dreams at that point to think that just five years later he would be nominated for his first Best Actor

Academy Award against Duvall's portrayal in *The Apostle*.

After the shoot was over, Matt packed up his saddle bags and headed back to Harvard to continue his pursuit of a college degree. "Each year I kept doing better and better," he recalls, "because I realized how great it was to be in school, how it gave me a kind of freedom that I may never have again in my whole life."

When *Geronimo* opened in December of 1993, Matt got his first taste of being at a big Hollywood premiere. His date for the event was girlfriend Schuyler Satinstein.

Finally, after three years at Harvard, the time came when Matt Damon had to decide between college and running away to California to pursue his acting full time. Finally it was "good-bye college" and "hello Hollywood." As he explains of his aborted college adventure, "I have another year to do, but I can't seem to schedule it in."

Brendan and Matt in a scene from *School Ties*.

His best buddy, Ben Affleck, had already packed his bags for Los Angeles, so they were reunited again. Oddly enough, after making the rounds of the auditions for quite some time, the first film that Matt landed was a movie that he and Ben appeared in together, *School Ties*. Also in the cast of *School Ties* were up-and-coming actors Chris O'Don-nell, Randall Batinkoff, Brendan Fraser, and Cole Hauser. The plot of *School Ties* centers on Brendan Fraser who portrays a 1950s Jewish student who wins a football scholarship to an Ivy League prep school. However, his dream school turns in a campus nightmare when he becomes the victim of anti-Semitism.

While Matt and Ben were busy on the set of their first major movie, *School Ties* in 1992, the auditions were announced for the film *Scent of a Woman*. According to Matt, "*Scent of a Woman* happened right during *School Ties*. The whole cast went down to audition for it. Chris O'Donnell was a business major at Boston College, and he's a very savvy businessman. So the way I found out about the

Matt had hoped that *School Ties* would bring him major stardom, but it did not.

Matt, Ben, and Chris O'Donnell portray Ivy League schoolboys in this story of intolerance.

part is, I'm checking in with my agent to see if anything good has come in, and my agent says, 'Here's one with a young role, and . . . Oh my God, it's got Al Pacino in it!' So I go up to Chris and say, 'Have you heard about this movie?' and he says, 'Yeah.' So I say, 'Do you have the script?' 'Yeah.' 'Can I see it?' 'No—I kinda need it.' Chris wouldn't give it to anybody. Later, Ben, me, Randall, Brendan, Anthony Rapp—we're all commiserating about our auditions, talking about how they didn't go well. Except for Chris. Chris used to play things close to the vest. We asked him how his audition went, and he just said, 'It was all right.' And we were like: 'Dude! Just tell us how it went!' And he would say, 'Ohhh, I don't know.'"

Although *School Ties* could have been the kind of film that would potentially turn Matt Damon into a star, it just didn't happen for him. According to him, "A lot of people got hot off that movie, but I wasn't one of them. I thought my performance was pretty good, but I didn't have a publicist, I didn't do many interviews and the phone just didn't ring."

Both he and Ben were hanging out with several of the hot young actors on the verge of having "happening" careers. Among his buddies at that time was Matthew McConaughey. When McConaughey landed the starring role as the Southern lawyer in the big-screen adaptation of John Grisham's *A Time to Kill*, opposite Ashley Judd, all of his friends were very excited and supportive. "When Matthew got *A Time to Kill*, we all went nuts. It was such a feeling of vindication—that one of our peer group, someone not on the A-list, got the part," says Matt.

While there has been a lot of talk about Damon's love affairs with some of the actresses with whom he later starred in films, during this same era in Los Angeles he had his first really serious girlfriend. "Not all of my girlfriends have been actresses," he reveals. "In fact, the love of my life was a doctor. We were college sweethearts. I was in L.A. and she was at Columbia—it was a long-distance romance, which was really hard. We did it for years, and then it was like the dynamic was becoming so f***ed up because we were trying to avoid the thing of not seeing each other for a long time and then being extra careful not to say something that might upset the other one. We decided to leave it to the gods—if it's meant to be, it's meant to be. And then she married someone else."

After *School Ties* Matt really expected his career to catch fire. Unfortunately it did not. Neither did the 1995 TV film *Good Old Boys*, nor the low-budget, short-lived comedy film that he and Ben appeared in called *Glory Daze*, which went unnoticed when it was released on September 27, 1996, and appeared on video a year later.

After all of this work, Matt was still a little further down the list of hot actors who were all trying out for the same parts. As he explains it, "If Brad Pitt, Johnny Depp, and Leonardo DiCaprio and every other name guy passed on a script, then maybe I would get the audition." It would still take a little more time and patience before the right role came along, but a great one was waiting just around the bend for him.

Finally, after three years at Harvard, the time came when Matt Damon had to decide between college and running away to California to pursue his acting full time.

Matt's Girls
The Women in Matt Damon's Life

Matt and Schuyler Satinstein.

Matt and Minnie Driver, lovers on screen and off.

At the *Courage Under Fire* premiere with Kara Sands.

After they were photographed together at the Golden Globe Awards, he was linked in the press with *Titanic* star Kate Winslett.

Matt on the town with his mom.

Actress Mary Kay Place raved about Matt after they co-starred in *The Rainmaker*.

Claire Danes and Matt had an off-camera affair amid the filming of *The Rainmaker*.

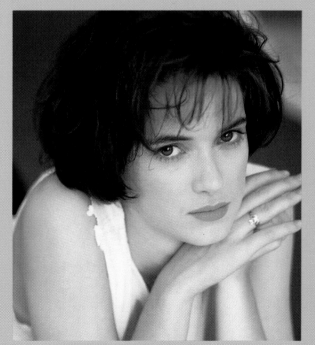

Matt's current girlfriend is Winona Ryder.

Starving for Attention

Meg Ryan and Matt Damon in *Courage Under Fire*.

A fter all of these on-camera experiences, Matt's career failed to heat up, and his phone wasn't ringing. Meanwhile, several of his actor buddies were moving up the ladder of the film world. "For me, I was sick of reading scripts that Chris O'Donnell had passed on, and I was looking for something to set me apart," he recalls.

Even Ben's younger brother, Casey, was having better luck with his career. Casey had been cast in the extremely popular black comedy *To Die For* (1995), which starred Nicole Kidman and was directed by Gus Van Sant. Since Matt was living on Ben and Casey's sofa at the time, they knew intimately what Damon's day-to-day

Matt was convinced
that the right role was
all he needed.

In *Courage Under Fire*, the events that followed this helicopter battle are replayed over and over again.

routine consisted of, and how demanding it was . . . or wasn't. Says Casey, "Basically Matt sat around, ate Cheerios, played video games, and scribbled in his notebook."

Finally a role came along that Matt auditioned for, and really wanted to sink his teeth into. It was the role of a drug-addicted and extremely self-destructive soldier in the early 1990s Gulf War, in the harrowing film *Courage Under Fire*. It starred Meg Ryan, Denzel Washington, and Lou Diamond Phillips.

Matt saw it as the kind of role that he could really make something out of, and he decided to dedicate all of his concentration toward landing it. "There's a very short list of young actors in Los Angeles," he recalls, "I thought this movie could help me climb a little higher in the pecking order."

Without consulting the director, Matt made the decision that the heroin-addicted character he portrayed should look emaciated, and on the verge of self-starvation. "It was a business decision. I thought, 'Nobody will take this

role, because it's too small. If I go out of my way to make something of this role . . .'" he pondered.

To say the least, Matt became fixated on taking this role and really making it dramatic and convincing. "I felt he should be a shell of a man at the end of the story," he says. "Not just because of the drugs he's been taking, but because of the guilt he feels has been eating away at him. It was the hardest thing I've ever had to do. I ran six miles in the morning and six miles at night, and I'd drink four to six pots of coffee to be able to run that distance. When I went into a restaurant, the first thing I would tell the waiters was, 'I'm your worst nightmare.' I wouldn't waver from my diet. It got so bad that when my girlfriend kissed me, I'd have to wash my mouth out because I could taste the oils on her lips from food she'd eaten."

He went on a strict "no sugar" and "no fat" diet, and 40 pounds began dropping off of him. "I was running 12 miles a day and not eating," he explains. "I killed myself for that role. I don't regret it, but I'd never do it again. I was getting dizzy and sick. I messed up my adrenal glands."

Admittedly, he took it a little too far. Even the director of the film, Edward Zwick, was shocked to see how thin Matt had become to prepare for the role. "He was scared, and he told me to start eating," Damon recalls.

Looking back on the experience, Matt laughs, "I was under two percent body fat. I remember seeing Lou Diamond Phillips and thinking, 'God, if I looked like that I wouldn't take my shirt off!' I thought he looked fat!"

His family was very concerned about him as well. According to his older brother Kyle, "He was obsessive about it. I'm genuinely worried about him. I know he will sacrifice himself for other people."

Matt's mother echoed her concern by explaining, "It was hard for me to go to the set of *Courage Under Fire*. I was deeply against the Gulf War, and I didn't know how the film was going to pan out politically."

Damon wanted to make sure that the Hollywood powers-that-be noticed him when they saw this highly praised and prestigious film. "'Look what I'll do, I'll kill myself!' Directors took note of it," he says.

Matt wasn't worried a bit about his health; he was more concerned with doing the best he

"I killed myself for that role. I don't regret it, but I'd never do it again."

could with this acting assignment, and performing in a cast of several Hollywood heavyweights with whom he was greatly impressed. "I tried to act unimpressed around Denzel Washington on *Courage Under Fire*," he recalls, "but one day I just couldn't help it. I started to quote [the film] *Malcolm X* (1992), the part where he talks about the chickens coming home to roost. He was so amazed—I think I knew more of it than he did!"

Lou Diamond Phillips explains, "It was amazing to watch his discipline. He kept to a diet of steamed chicken breast and

Matt's co-star Lou Diamond Phillips admired the way he went to extremes to bring his character realistically to the screen.

The drama of *Courage Under Fire* was set against the Gulf War of the early 1990s.

steamed vegetables, and that's it. Matt likes to eat, so this was a huge undertaking for him."

After filming was underway, it seemed that everyone in the cast was trying to get him to eat something, they were so concerned about his health. "By that point I was so far gone that I wasn't going to compromise," Matt claimed. "I'm not sorry I did it. I knew it was a great role with a real chance to do something I hadn't done before. I just didn't know the effects would be so long-lasting. I went to a doctor in Boston after I got back from shooting and he said, 'The good news is that your heart didn't shrink.' But my blood sugar was all messed up, and I'm still on medication to correct that."

In the plot of the film *Courage Under Fire*, Denzel Washington portrays Nat Serling, a Gulf War veteran who is investigating a potential posthumous Medal of Honor recipient. While doing his investigation, he interviews each of the soldiers who were under the command of a remarkable female soldier, Captain Karen Walden, portrayed by Meg Ryan. Amongst them was medical officer, Ilario, portrayed by Damon. In the scenes in which Matt is interviewed by Washington, he looks gaunt, skinny, and unattractive in an emaciated way.

He appears to be a mere shadow of himself.

During Damon's character's testimony, he becomes flustered and uncertain of his story. He has trouble sitting still, looking very much like a junkie worried where his next fix is coming from. Matt wanted to look believably like a shell of the man who had gone off to war, and his appearance and his very connected performance brilliantly portrayed this dramatic dilemma.

There were also several harrowing combat sequences in which Matt, Meg, Lou, and the rest of the crew are shown crashing a helicopter and dodging machine-gun cross fire. Hopefully the filming of these sequences made up for all of those years of Damon being forbidden to play with guns as a kid.

Courage Under Fire again found Matt Damon walking up the red carpet at a big gala Hollywood premiere. He was all smiles as he strode up to the theater arm in arm with his girlfriend at the time, Kara Sands.

In the end, his hard work and dedication paid off, with critics and the media unanimously praising his performance. Steven Farber in *Movieline* magazine raved about "Matt Damon's shattering perfor-

A gaunt Matt Damon breaks down when he is questioned by Denzel Washington.

mance in the film," concluding, "Damon provided much of the soul of *Courage Under Fire*." David Blum in *Newsweek* glowingly announced, "His breakthrough came as a Gulf War veteran turned heroin addict. . . . The intensity of his performance convinced the industry that Damon was a serious actor." And, Justine Elias in *US* magazine claimed, "His most notable work has been his devastating performance as a haunted, drug-addicted Persian Gulf War veteran in *Courage Under Fire*."

Now that he had proven that he could not only hold his own in a cast filled with top-notch actors, Matt Damon needed to land a job that was really going to showcase his talent, and utilize him as a leading character. He was about to win just such a role.

Matt Hits His Stride

Matt's big break came when he landed the role of Rudy Baylor in *The Rainmaker*.

In spite of the great notices he received in the press, Matt's performance in *Courage Under Fire* didn't turn him into a bankable star. Again he found himself making the rounds of the casting calls, looking for work. Matt found himself passed by for role after role during this era. One of the big-budget films that he auditioned for was the prestigious *Batman Forever*, a production in search of the perfect Robin.

"I'd have taken Robin," he reveals. "Hell, I auditioned for it. When they first offered it to Chris O'Donnell he wanted more money, so they had auditions and I did a screen test for Joel Schumacher. *Primal Fear*—you know the Edward Norton role? It more or less came down to him and me, and he pretty much put a smokin' on me. *To Die For* I lost nearly 20 pounds to audition for, but Wock [Joaquin Phoenix] got it."

Then there was his personal life, which was

Matt and Danny DeVito in *The Rainmaker*.

also floundering. He had become engaged to his college girlfriend, who attended Columbia University. As he explains it, "My engagement hadn't worked out, so I was living with our other buddy, Soren." At the time, Ben Affleck had also broken up with his current girlfriend, and he was in residence on Soren's sofa. Nothing seemed to be happening for either Matt or Ben.

It was around this same time that Matt and Ben began using some of their vastly abundant spare time to work on the screenplay that would become *Good Will Hunting*. According to Damon, "For five years or so; our bank accounts would get down to the point where we needed to get a job and another job would come along—although it wasn't always a lot of money."

They both figured that they had nothing to lose. "We wrote it right out of frustration," Matt admits. "It was like, 'Why are we sitting here? Let's make our own movie. And if people come to see it, they come; and if they don't, they don't. Either way it beats sitting here going crazy.' When you have so much energy and so much

passion and no outlet for it and nobody cares, it's just the worst feeling. And there are hundreds of thousands of people like that in L.A. right now. This whole 'I'm too cool to care' thing you get among young actors in this country is so weak and stupid and played out, and it just brings everybody down. You shouldn't be too cool to care, for Christ's sake. You should be full of vim and vigor, and trying to do everything you can to make a change."

Meanwhile, the audition for a powerful role in a film came along, and Matt gave it his all. Cast as the lead character, Rudy Baylor, in Francis Ford Coppola's production of *The Rainmaker*, Matt again threw himself fully into the movie. When Matthew McConaughey starred in John Grisham's *A Time to Kill* (1996) as a young Southern lawyer up against the system, it had turned him into a major star. Now that Matt was cast as another young Southern lawyer up against the system in the screen adaptation of yet another John Grisham novel, it seemed like a "shoo in" that *The Rainmaker* would attract the same kind of career-building attention to Damon. Unfortunately, it did not.

First of all, the film's incredible Hollywood all-star cast included

Claire Danes, Danny DeVito, John Voight, Mary Kay Place, Roy Scheider, Mickey Rourke, and Alfred Hitchcock film veteran Theresa Wright. While Matt was in great company, and he turned in an appealingly believable characterization, it was not to become a star-making turn for him.

The women in the cast found him especially charming to be around during the filming of the movie. Mary Kay Place, who first became a star in the hit 1970s TV series *Mary Hartman, Mary Hartman*, played the part of the mother of a cancer victim whom a crooked insurance company turns their back on. As a fellow actor, Mary Kay was very verbal about how impressed she was to have worked with Damon. Very often, an actor can only deliver a great performance if he or she has a strong actor to play a scene against. She found Matt to be very

generous and giving in their scenes together, which became some of the film's strongest sequences.

Says Place, "The thing that kills me about Matt is he works more than anybody in the film, 16 hours a day for four and one half months. And you never heard him get irritable or complain—and you could see he was exhausted. He's generous beyond belief, both to the crew and the cast. He has a

Damon finds himself defending a family against a crooked insurance company.

huge heart, this guy."

Being from Boston, several of the Southern cast and crew members were impressed with the job Matt did coming up with a believable regional accent. Pamela Chapman, who played the role of Vera Birdsong in the film, proclaimed, "I couldn't believe he was from the North because he had such extremely good manners."

Ann Marie Caskey, the assistant casting director for the film, admittedly had a major crush on him. She was also thrilled to find that he flirted back with her. "But then," she confessed, "I realized he was just trying to catch on to my Memphis accent."

The one female member of the cast who was truly swept off her feet by Damon's performance on and off camera was Claire Danes. Best known for her portrayal of Juliet opposite Leonardo DiCaprio in *Romeo + Juliet*, in this film Danes played a battered wife who finally reached the last straw in her relationship with her husband. Reportedly, she and Matt had quite a strong love affair off the set.

Matt was truly impressed with

Claire Danes plays a woman who is finally pushed over the emotional edge by her abusive husband.

the fact that he now had the chance to work with the legendary producer Frances Ford Coppola. According to Matt, "The guy's a f***ing genius, pure and simple. Working with him was wonderful. Everyone had a ball."

After they were done with the principal photography on the film, work had begun on the post-production side of the process, which included overdubbing vocals, and putting finishing touches to several of the scenes. According to Matt, "I went to San Francisco to do some post-production stuff on *The Rainmaker*, and one night there was a premiere for the re-release of *The Godfather*. I went with Danny DeVito, and sat with him and [Paramount movie executive] Sherry Lansing. I had never seen it on the big screen, because I was only two when the movie came out. Before the film started I said to Sherry, 'This is so cool. I've never seen it on the big screen.' She looks at the guy next to her and says, 'See Al, Matt's never seen it either.' Then Al Pacino peeks around Sherry and says, 'You've never seen it on the big screen? Me either. I saw it on TV, but never on the big screen.' I was so stunned to be looking Al Pacino in the face, I just said, 'Well, it's good, and you did a good job.'

Danny DeVito tries to show Matt the ropes, when he takes on his first big case.

Ben Affleck and Joey Lauren Adams in *Chasing Amy*, a film that also featured Matt Damon.

Then I kinda leaned back in my chair and felt like such a putz."

When *The Rainmaker* was released in 1997, Matt drew praise for his portrayal of the lead character. Robert Schickel in *Time* magazine wrote, "Matt Damon has cornered the always busy market in youthful, affronted innocence . . . playing Rudy Baylor, the young, undertrained lawyer trying his first case, he shows a nice sneaky

knuckler, tracking an erratic path toward the strike zone." Barbara Shulgasser of the *San Francisco Examiner* claimed, "Damon reveals a storehouse of deep emotion and considerable poise for someone so young."

Around the same time, Ben Affleck was cast as the star of the third film in the trilogy that includes *Clerks* (1994) and *Mall-rats* (1995). It was called *Chasing*

Amy (1997). In addition, both Ben's younger brother Casey and Matt Damon have very small supporting roles in the film. *Chasing Amy* was really Ben Affleck's first major star turn. He starred as one half of a successful comic book artist team. Ben's character becomes all befuddled when he discovers that the beautiful, vivacious girl he falls in love with is a lesbian. He does everything he can to turn the situation around, including suggesting a three-way love affair with his writing partner. Matt portrays the role of a film-maker who tries to sell Ben and his partner a deal to turn the comic book into a film. Damon's appearance in *Chasing Amy* only lasts half a minute, so you have to pay close attention to the screen to catch him. Ben, however, emerges a highly appealing leading man in this off-beat, quirky comedy-of-errors film about twentysomething adults in New Jersey and Manhattan in the mixed-up 1990s.

However you sliced it, Matt Damon and his buddy Ben Affleck were on their way to big things. The March 1997 issue of *Movieline* magazine forecast what was in the young actor's near future by stating: "After *Rainmaker*, Damon will star in a film he wrote himself." Talk about an understatement! But then again, who could predict what a huge hit *Good Will Hunting* was to become.

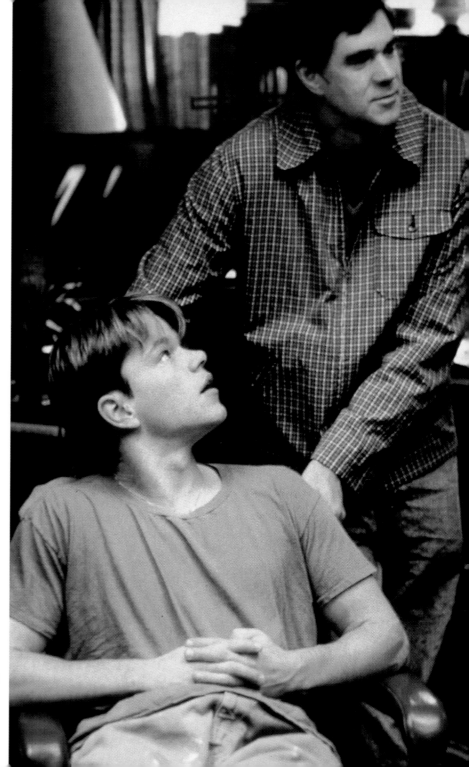

Matt, looking up to *Good Will Hunting* director Gus Van Sant.

In Good Company

The Other Men Nominated Alongside Matt Damon for the 1998 Best Actor Academy Award

Dustin Hoffman for *Wag the Dog*

Peter Fonda for *Ulee's Gold*

Robert Duvall for *The Apostle*

Jack Nicholson for *As Good As It Gets*

When Matt was nominated for an Academy Award in the category of Best Actor in *Good Will Hunting*, he was in distinguished company. Ultimately, Jack Nicholson took home the trophy.

The Writing of a Hit

Finally, Matt decided to sit down and write himself the ultimate film role.

It was out of sheer frustration and blind determination that the script and the inevitable hit film *Good Will Hunting* was born. During the filming of all the aforementioned projects in the past couple of years—including *School Ties*, *Chasing Amy*, and *Glory Daze*—Matt and Ben were working on a whole new project of their own to star in, which would show off their talents as actors, and ultimately as screenplay writers.

As Damon explains, "The truth is we couldn't get arrested as actors, so we thought, 'Why don't we just write our own movie?' At the time Ben was sleeping on my couch. We were desperate."

All in all, the writing, selling, and filming of what would become *Good Will Hunting*, would take up five years of their time, in between all of the other projects. Even when they were geographically separated, by school or by separate

Landing Robin Williams for *Good Will Hunting* was a real coup for the project.

movie locations, Matt and Ben kept writing and revising their creation. "Once we started," Matt explains, "we really got into a groove. While I was away, I'd write and fax the stuff to Ben, and Ben would fax stuff to me, and we'd write on and edit each other's faxes. It was basically the same as sitting in a room saying, 'No, no. I think you should say *that*.'"

The script itself came out in chunks. They would write a large piece of it, and then some other project would arise, so they would put it on "hold," and then return to working on it. "After about a year, Ben and I started talking one night, and the script began flowing right out. Then we wrote it very fast," says Matt.

They not only wrote roles for themselves in the screenplay, they also wrote several parts for their actor friends, including Ben's little brother Casey. "When those guys wrote *Good Will Hunting*, they wrote me into it. And they didn't have to," a grateful Casey Affleck proclaims. "So they've been very inclusive. I think when people have that attitude, there's just no room for competition, because someone is saying they're willing to give."

According to Matt, "The hardest part was putting the story together. We finally realized that

you're supposed to have something *happen* when you write a movie, so we improvised a few dramatic scenes for good measure."

Ben laughingly admits, "Then we looked over a few encyclopedias to make ourselves sound more intelligent."

Describing their writing skills as a team, Matt explains, "It wasn't like someone was good at structure and someone at dialogue. The only difference between us is Ben can type."

This was a whole new experience for the duo. "We never fancied ourselves writers," Damon admits. "And actually, it was a source of embarrassment for us when we sold the script, because a lot of our friends really are writers and can write a lot better than we can, except maybe dialogue. Writing a script is different, though, because to me it's not really writing. It's acting, is what it is. We still don't call ourselves writers. We just kind of go, 'Well, I guess that worked.'"

Originally, the story was much more complicated. Instead of centering all of its action on the characters of Will (Matt Damon) and his construction worker buddy Chuckie (Ben Affleck), and the dilemma of a college education, it had a subplot involving intrigue at

NASA (National Aeronautics and Space Administration). Instead of the mentor/professor whom actor Stellan Skarsgård plays, his role was that of an FBI agent. That was the state it was in when Matt and Ben began shopping it around to the major movie studios. Much to their surprise, they found a lot of people who were interested in their script.

"It was the first time we realized how Hollywood works," Matt reveals. "We'd both gone in for a lot of auditions, but when you actually have something that people are trying to buy from you, it's a whole different thing."

The week of November 13, 1994, will be remembered as the week of the big studio bidding frenzy. "It literally turned into a four-day event. It started on a Monday, and by the Thursday night there was an all-out bidding war for the script," Matt recalls.

At the time of the script auction, Ben and Matt were living on sandwiches made of the infamous canned processed meat know as Spam. They had both achieved flashes of success, but both of them were between gigs at the time.

Robin was very impressed with Matt, both as an actor and as a screenplay writer too.

> ## "Oh, man, when we finally sold the script, we had everybody over to our house. It was warm Pabst Blue Ribbon beer for everybody!"

"When the phone started ringing, we were ready to take the first offer, which was $15,900." Ben Affleck recalls.

"After each call," says Damon, "We were yelling at our agent Patrick Whitesell, 'Take it! Just take the offer!' Then there was this moment when the phone rang and [my roommate] Patrick picked it up. It was for my roommate, and it was this girl he had dated in college, and my roommate was, like, 'Hey, how are you?' And we were, like, 'Hang the f***in' phone up!' He was really bummed, because they hadn't talked in three years."

When the smoke cleared that evening, it was Castle Rock Pictures who had outbid the rest of the competition. In the final tally, Castle Rock's bid that evening was in the vicinity of $1 million.

That was the day the boys went from eating Spam to dining on steaks. Damon laughs, "When this bidding war happened, we were just f***ing 'Spamming' it. Within three days, they had given us so f***ing much money, we didn't even know what to do. One of my actor friends came over and read about us on the front page of *Variety*, and he goes, 'We're going to the Sizzler like a motherf***er.' That was it. We just got in the car and went to Sizzler."

That night was cause for a huge celebration. "Oh, man, when we finally sold the script, we had everybody over to our house. It was warm Pabst Blue Ribbon [beer] for everybody!" Matt recalls.

Were they ever afraid that the whole project was just going to blow up in their faces, or turn into a huge embarrassment? "We were afraid on a human level," Matt confirms. "We were talking about the difference between eating Spam every day and being able to buy a three-bedroom house with a pool table and new cars. So here we are, and we sell the script to Castle Rock."

One of the major elements of

Minnie Driver dazzles in *Good Will Hunting*.

the deal was the contractual clause that insisted that Matt and Ben would portray the lead roles as the Bostonian best friends. The on-screen relationship between those two characters very closely paralleled their own real-life friendship. The contractual ploy was a similar move that Stallone pulled when he sold the original script for *Rocky*. According to Damon, "Sylvester Stallone set the precedent that allowed us to do this."

Not everyone found this an appealing aspect to the deal. "A lot of places turned it down," says Matt. "Everybody who bid said they'd pay more if they were free not to cast us. We felt we had nothing to lose."

However, once the ink had dried on the contracts, both Matt and Ben found they weren't exactly out of the woods. Castle Rock wanted to implement some changes in the script and the direction of the film immediately. Rob Reiner, the director who is also a partner in Castle Rock, wanted them to drop the NASA adventure angle to the plot of the film, and to center the emotional core of the film on the friendship between Will and Chuckie. This ultimately became a good thing in the long run.

"We had really serious cre-

As Will Hunting, Matt struggles to define his life.

ative differences with them," Matt recalls of their clashes with Castle Rock. After a very heated meeting, only 63 pages of the original script remained intact. The instant dream project led to a year full of rewrites in which the plot of the script went through several changes. In one version, Chuckie was killed by a falling construction beam. In another rendition, Sean the therapist became Chuckie's construction site foreman-turned-therapist.

When Matt and Ben took the new, improved and approved version of the script back to Castle Rock in October of 1995, there erupted a huge creative impasse. Castle Rock insisted that the film be directed by Andrew Schein-

man. At that point, Scheinman's only directorial credit was the flop film *Little Big League* (1994), which starred Timothy Busfield. Damon and Affleck freaked out, opposing this move. There were also several other creative issues that the duo disliked. Instead of telling them to "go fly a kite," Castle Rock cut a deal with them. If they could get another studio to buy out their contract in 30 days, they would allow them to do so. If they did not, then Castle Rock had the rights to assign any director to the project that they saw fit.

Matt and Ben basically had to go out on their own and find another buyer who would absorb all of Castle Rock's costs. Says Affleck, "It had the curse of being

Portraying best friends on camera came naturally for Ben and Matt.

in turnaround, and now [we] had a reputation for being difficult."

It was serious "back to the drawing board time" for the duo. If they failed to come up with a buyer, they could get written out of the deal as actors. "So we sat down with Chris Moore, our producer, and said, 'What are we going to do?'" Ben recalls. "Thanks to Chris, Miramax came to the rescue."

Much to their surprise and delight, Harvey Weinstein of Miramax Pictures bailed them out. According to Harvey, "We stuck with Ben and Matt when nobody wanted them. Other studios wouldn't make the movie with them. Even once I agreed to make the movie, everyone kept saying, 'Look, I can get you big stars.' Some big-name directors turned it down because we went with those actors. It was totally insane to put two completely unknown guys in these main roles."

Now the next element to fall into place was finding the right director. "We got to Miramax's offices just before our lunch," Matt says, "and Harvey tells us, 'Mel Gibson is a great director. You can see that from *Braveheart*.' And I said, 'Harvey, Ben and I have been working. We haven't seen it yet.' So without missing a beat, the head of Miramax sits there and says, 'Okay: Scotland, William Wallace.' And he told us the whole movie."

Unfortunately Mel was tied up for a year and a half while working on the film *Ransom*. Ben and Matt couldn't wait that long to get this project into production. According to Damon, "Mel was totally understanding when we said, 'This movie is our life. And we know you're like, the biggest star in the world. But we need a decision.'"

Ultimately, Mel Gibson was unable to shift his commitments around. Enter: Gus Van Sant, who is best known for his off-beat films like *To Die For* and *Drugstore Cowboy*.

According to Ben Affleck, "Gus Van Sant knew of us—my brother had acted in *To Die For* (1995)—and we heard he wanted to direct *Good Will Hunting*. We loved the idea, because we respect him so much. Gus has this way of

delivering earth-shattering news in the most disarming, nonflustered flat monotone. 'Yeah, I want to direct it,' he said. 'That's if you want to do it. Okay? Bye.' So, as Ben said, 'Fortune was in favor of us fools'—and we're happy!"

Furthermore, they were relieved to have a director assigned to the project who had a strong sense of what the finished film project could grow to become. As Ben put it, "We knew it wouldn't be a

movie by committee. It wouldn't be watered down. It would be a Gus Van Sant movie."

Against all odds, Damon and Affleck had their dream movie in the works. They had a script that everyone agreed upon, they were going to star in it, and they had one of the most cutting edge directors signed to the deal. As Matt so eloquently states, "It was our way of saying, 'Screw the system. We're doing our own thing!'"

The Filming of a Dream

Now that they were working with a really strong script, and a well-respected director, what they needed was a couple of real box-office drawing stars to appear in the film. Since both Matt and Ben were relative "unknowns," attaching a famous name to the project was a crucial element toward assuring that the movie would be a hit. According to Matt, "We learned from *Reservoir Dogs* (1992) that once [producer-director] Quentin Tarantino got Harvey Keitel, that got the movie made."

Enter: Robin Williams. "I just knew that it was a well-written piece. When you have that, it's a running start," Robin says of the original shooting script. "To me it was just an extraordinary script. It was quite shocking when I met

Bringing *Good Will Hunting* to the screen was a five-year project for Matt.

Ben and Matt's on-screen chemistry in *Good Will Hunting* gave the film heart.

Matt and Ben and saw how young they were—I was like 'May I see some ID?'"

Next came the casting of the female lead character, Skylar. When a beautiful brunette named Minnie Driver showed up, Matt Damon just lit up. Besides being perfect for the part of the aloof girl who wins the heart of the character Will Hunting, Minnie also shared a dedication to her craft above and beyond the call of duty. While Matt lost 40 pounds to look gauntly thin for *Courage Under Fire*, Minnie had to gain 40 pounds to star in the critically acclaimed *Circle of Friends* (1995). "It was about the same amount of weight," Matt says with

empathy. "She's very dedicated to her work and that's beautiful. That's always the first thing that attracts me to somebody, to see them be so passionate about something." Everyone knew right then and there that Minnie was absolutely perfect for the role, and she was awarded the role of Skylar.

With the cast and director now in place, filming began on April 14, 1997. Describing the action, Matt explains the story of fictional character Will Hunting: "He's an orphan, a born genius, who's discovered working as a janitor at MIT [Massachusetts Institute of Technology], and it's about him being caught between all

these different worlds: the world of his friends; the world of the therapist [Robin Williams] he comes in contact with; the world of this really amazing woman [Minnie Driver] he meets who challenges him; and then there's the lure of the world his genius introduces him to, which is represented by this math professor [Stellan Skarsgård]. So he has to face all these different forces that are at work. It's like a comedy and a drama and a coming-of-age story."

According to him, "If the movie has any message, it's 'Don't regret what you didn't do. Beat your head against that wall. At least you'll have tried.'"

The first major scene that was filmed was one led by Williams. Matt will never forget the emotional moment when he actually heard the words he and Ben had penned coming out of Robin's mouth. "By the time they said 'action,' tears were running down my face. I looked over at Ben and he was the same way. Then right after the scene, Robin came over and put his hands on our heads and said, 'It's not a fluke; you guys really did it.'"

Co-producer Chris Moore echoes that same emotional event by stating, "There was this meaningful moment, [where] Damon and Affleck realized, 'We are making this movie, and that is Robin Williams over there saying the lines that we wrote.'"

Robin found himself completely caught up in the significance of the moment. "They had this dream a long time ago, and it finally was happening," he said with a smile.

Matt was thrilled to share some of the most important scenes in the film with Robin. "I had to say the whole speech in two breaths. One wrong word and it was a retake. Robin Williams likened the scene to doing stand-up [comedy]. 'Stop and you die,' he said."

Matt and Ben had nothing but wonderful things to say about Gus Van Sant's direction of their film. Van Sant is known in some circles

Cole Hauser, Casey Affleck, Matt Damon, and Ben Affleck.

Minnie and Matt were convincing as lovers—on screen and off.

as being very controversial, and is someone who likes to "push the envelope" when it comes to edgy material, as he did with *My Own Private Idaho* (1991), his tawdry tale of male prostitutes in the Northwest. According to Damon, "He's like a church mouse, extra-ordinarily perceptive and quiet. [He] really nurtures his actors."

And then there was the on-screen/off-screen romance that took place between Matt Damon and Minnie Driver. "I fell in love with her," Matt said in 1997. "I don't think either one of us took the characters home with us. But, I am careful about talking about it. I don't want anything to detract from the work she did in the movie. She's a magnificent actress."

Although they both had very busy careers and personal lives, Matt felt that he and Minnie really had a chance at making something of their personal relationship. All of a sudden they were seen all over Hollywood, as two co-stars very much in love. According to Damon at the time, "We really have to work at it, but if we want it, we can have it. I really feel that way. Maybe it's naive. I have a lot of work ahead of me this year, but I really want to have that relationship. She's awesome."

Aside from brilliant casting, one of the key aspects in the plot of the movie centers around the large chalkboards with challenging equations to be solved written on them, outside of the classrooms. A janitor at this Boston-area institute of higher learning, the character of Will Hunting, is able to solve these mathematic problems with ease. Matt explained how he learned about them and made them a significant part of the plot of the film. "My sister-in-law works at M.I.T., and visiting her, I discovered they have chalkboards in the hallways. These chalkboards play an important role in a pivotal scene."

One of the things that Matt especially wanted to ring true in this film were the Bostonian accents. Duplicating the speech patterns of natives of the city nicknamed "bean town" is no easy task. "No one has ever accurately played a Boston accent, much less the cultural aspect of the city," Matt claims. "Actors start doing a weird Kennedy/Brahmin thing. Robert Mitchum came close in *The Friends of Eddie Coyle* (1973). You've got to be from there to do it. I don't even think Meryl Streep could do it." So accurately Boston is *Good Will Hunting* that in one of the outdoor restaurant scenes, two prominent Bostonians—both Matt's and Ben's mothers—were featured on camera.

When the filming of *Good Will Hunting* was underway, everyone who had anything to do with it

And then there was the on-screen/off-screen romance that took place between Matt Damon and Minnie Driver.

was certain that it was going to become a huge hit when it was released. Probably the biggest compliment of all came from Robin Williams when he proclaimed, "There's an emotional core to *Good Will Hunting* that came from Ben and Matt. They have this unspoken twins thing. They care for each other, yet they bust on each other. And that was a great bass line to work with. I'm very proud of this movie. It has a resonance."

And the Winner Is...

Minnie, Matt, and Ben.

In June of 1997 the principal photography for *Good Will Hunting* was completed, and director Gus Van Sant and editor Pietro Scalia set about the task of editing the raw footage. Prior to the film's release, Van Sant announced that he had received an overwhelmingly favorable response from everyone he had previewed it for. "I haven't really had anyone I've shown it to not like the film, which is really unusual for me," he explained at the time. "I guess that before, I felt that portraying something out of the mainstream was a powerful way of telling a story. But this time the story itself was enough."

The official American release date of the film was set for December 5. Two days later, on December 7, 1997, the film opened in Boston, Massachusetts, at a special Harvard Square gala, where Matt Damon and Ben Affleck were treated to an old-fashioned hometown Hollywood-style premiere. They were surrounded by a tight circle of family and friends. The post-premiere party was held at a local Irish pub by the name of The Burren. It was clearly a "local boys make good" kind of event.

This was Matt and Ben's "baby," and no one was more thrilled than they were about the finished film, and all of the excitement. According to Matt, "I'll never forget the first time we saw the movie at the premiere, looking at the faces of the people who were behind this movie. I'm very aware of who was there when I needed them, when I was completely powerless and begging. Believe me, we know every single person who was behind this movie, and every single person who wasn't."

The reviews were unanimously strong from the very start. According to David Ansen and Jeff Giles in *Newsweek* magazine, "To see the rich and funny *Good Will Hunting* is to know, inside of just two or

Damon, in the winner's circle.

> **What is the secret to maintaining a friendship such as theirs? According to Ben, it is quite a simple formula: "We're not competitive."**

three scenes, why Damon has become Hollywood's undisputed Young Man of the Moment . . . he's sensationally convincing and appealing as this whiz kid, a fascinating mixture of aggression, sweetness, hurt and intellectual bravado." Giving the film three and a half stars out of four, Mike Clark in *USA Today* proclaimed, "Matt Damon . . . delivers the year's No. 1 break-

through performance directly atop his agreeable high-profile turn in John Grisham's *The Rainmaker*—both after a career of nearly a decade's duration. Damon convincingly matches [Robin] Williams recrimination for recrimination in this portrayal of mutual tough love."

Fame so often brings unexpected pressures to one's life. Such was the case with Matt's love affair

with Minnie Driver. As the film heated up at the box-office in December of 1997, their relationship was very swiftly deteriorating. When Matt and Ben appeared on Oprah Winfrey's TV show on January 12, 1998, Damon announced, "I care about her a lot. We kind of decided it wasn't meant to be."

That month at the annual Golden Globe Awards presentation, Matt and Minnie reportedly clung to opposite sides of the room, not wanting to be seen or photographed together. Apparently, their break-up was something less than cordial.

Directly afterward, Matt was reportedly dating Winona Ryder. They had been introduced to each other by Gwyneth Paltrow, Ben Affleck's girlfriend of the moment.

Since Matt was nominated for Best Actor in *Good Will Hunting*, and Kate Winslet was nominated for Best Actress for her starring role in *Titanic*, getting them in the same frame of film seemed like a perfect "photo opportunity." When the photos ran in the newspapers and tabloids, reporters speculated that Matt was having an affair with Kate. "I can't believe it!" he exclaimed after the Golden Globe Awards. "I got romantically linked to Kate Winslet! What she really did was say, 'If you're ever in London,

At the premiere of *Good Will Hunting*.

Winning the Golden Globe for the screenplay of *Good Will Hunting*, January 18, 1998.

give me a call.' They made it sound like it was possibly a tryst. . . . I talked to her after that article came out, and I told her we got linked. We were both laughing. She thought it was really cool."

When the nominations for the Academy Awards were announced in January of 1998, it was like hitting the "gold rush." *Good Will Hunting* received an impressive number of nine separate nominations: Best Picture; Best Actor, Matt Damon; Best Supporting Actor, Robin Williams; Best Supporting Actress, Minnie Driver; Best Director, Gus Van Sant; Best Screenplay (written for the screen), Matt Damon and Ben Affleck; Best Dramatic Score, Danny Elfman; Best Original Song, "Miss Misery," written by Elliott Smith; and Best Film Editing. When the nominations were offi-

cially announced, Matt was completely "blown away" by this avalanche of acceptance and honor. "I can't even comprehend this," he claimed dumbfoundedly.

When Matt heard the big news, who was the first person he called on the telephone to share the announcement? "My first call when I got the news was to Ben," he recalls. "Then my mother, my father, my brother, in that order."

Accepting their Oscars on stage in front of a television viewing audience of millions of people around the world.

Of all of the awards *Good Will Hunting* was up for, it was the Best Screenplay one that impressed him the most. "The writing nomination is the most amazing kind of accomplishment," he says. "It took five years out of my life and Ben's. We were told 'no' by so many people in so many rooms. Every studio had a chance."

Since they won the Golden Globe Award in the category of Best Original Screenplay, several reporters began asking them if that would be Matt and Ben's new area of concentration, as opposed to acting. According to Damon,

"Neither of us really long to be screenwriters, but at the same time, that would be a category in which we'd be nominated together. I don't care if we were nominated for Best Morons, because I'd think, 'Well I got nominated with Ben, and that's pretty cool. . . . If you put us together, you might actually make a whole, creative interesting individual. We're a lot like the Wonder Twins."

Then, on top of that, came the crowning honor of being in the running for Best Actor. Being nominated for his acting alongside such well-established legends as

Robert Duvall, Dustin Hoffman, Jack Nicholson, and Peter Fonda really touched Matt. Just to be mentioned in the same paragraph as these acting legends made him speechless with emotion. As he explained prior to the awards telecast, "I don't know how to sound. I'm afraid this will sound disingenuous, but it really is a serious moment in my life."

In the months between the December 7, 1997 release of *Good Will Hunting* and the March 23, 1998 presentation of the Academy Awards, it seemed like the media blitz over Matt was off and running. For a cover story feature piece in *Vanity Fair* magazine, Damon was dressed in designer duds and photographed by lens master Bruce Weber. Making fun of the high-fashion fuss that was made over him in front of the cameras, he laughed over the fact that his usual outfit was either khakis or jeans. "I went to Calvin Klein," he said with a smile. "They tried all these things on me and said I looked very 'fash.' They promised me that I'll look 'fash.'"

When he was flown in to New York City and put up at the swanky Four Seasons Hotel, he found himself in a suite on the 43rd floor, with a fully stocked refrigerator and a view to die for.

He had come a long way from sleeping on the sofa and eating everyone's favorite "mystery meat"—Spam. When he was interviewed by Martha Frankel of *Movieline* magazine, he laughed, "My assistant and I got here last night and we felt just like 'The Jeffersons!' We were saying, 'How did we end up in this place?' Then we hit the minibar and ate everything in it. I kept saying, 'We're not paying for any of this sh**, right?"

In a special issue of the *Hollywood Reporter* in March of 1998, several key film industry people were interviewed about Damon's drawing power at the box-office. According to Jim Woodin of Edwards Cinema, "Matt garnered lots of name recognition for *The Rainmaker*. People coming to the theater to see the film referred to it as 'that Matt Damon picture.'

Matt, Robin, and Ben: an Oscar-winning trio.

Academy Award Nominations For Good Will Hunting

Best Picture

Best Actor,
Matt Damon

Best Supporting Actor,
Robin Williams

Best Supporting Actress,
Minnie Driver

Best Director,
Gus Van Sant

Best Screenplay
(written for the screen), Matt
Damon and Ben Affleck

Best Dramatic Score,
Danny Elfman

Best Original Song,
"Miss Misery," written by
Elliott Smith

Best Film Editing

Damon's boy-next-door quality appeals to audiences and he appears very comfortable on the screen."

In the same issue, Bob Laemmle of Laemmle Theatres claimed, "It's very simple: he makes good choices and he's been in good films. And in *Hunting*, audiences have found a connection with the dialogue—it's superb."

Everything was suddenly coming up "Matt Damon" right and left. He had gone from getting the hand-me-down scripts to bona fide A-list treatment. Now everyone in Hollywood wanted him to star in their next film.

When the Academy Awards were handed out, and Matt and Ben were handed their trophies for writing the screenplay for

Good Will Hunting, all of Hollywood was on their feet cheering them on. These two young upstart kids had put their dream movie down on paper, somehow gotten it produced, and now they were in the winner's circle.

Matt Damon had finally arrived!

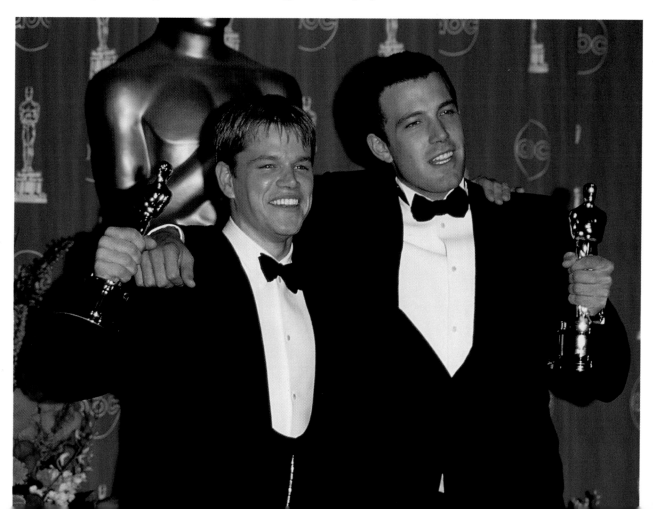

The Talented Mr. Damon

Matt at the V-Day 1998 benefit, in New York City.

N o one was more thrilled and excited about his newfound fame and acceptance than Matt Damon himself. As he admitted with amazement, "I'm knocking on wood so hard my knuckles are bleeding. I cannot believe any of this."

It seemed inevitable that his life was about to go through some major changes because of everything that had happened to him. "It is a whole new world. I don't mind if my life changes. The question is: 'Change into what?' There are a lot of people I see who get celebrity and end up being pretty lonely. They end up raping and pillaging the temptations. They end up standing there in

The harrowing war drama, *Saving Private Ryan*, is Matt's summer 1998 film.

middle age saying, 'What the hell happened?' I would not want to live like that. There's a part of me that wants to have that smaller, manageable, 'normal' life."

One of his biggest fans is Robin Williams. Because of *Good Will Hunting*, Robin snagged the Oscar that had eluded him for the past several years. Speaking of Matt, Williams glowingly reported, "He makes fun of it himself. He's going to do great."

Although it appears that his fame is a matter of "overnight success," looking at it from the inside, Damon views it quite differently. "I feel like it's been gradual," he says. "I've walked down the red carpet for *School Ties*, *Geronimo*, and *Courage Under Fire*, and everyone's going, 'Matt! Matt! Over here!' and they're taking pictures. And the first two movies bombed. It was a real lesson in humility. That stuff is all so f***ing fleeting,

you know? A few years ago, I would have told you that it should have happened for me then. But I'm glad it happened this way. It does give me more perspective. I'd like to think that, anyway."

Because of the success of *The Rainmaker* and *Good Will Hunting*, Matt's status in the business went from "so unknown he couldn't get arrested" to "unbelievably hot." For the first time ever, his acting services were being fought over by two different directors at once. The first offer was from director Ang Lee, who was famed for his prestigious hit films *Sense and Sensibility* (1995) and *The Ice Storm* (1997). Lee was casting his Civil War epic, *To Live Again*, and he wanted Damon to star opposite pop-star-turned-actress Jewel. At the same time Anthony Minghella was pursuing Matt to star in his upcoming film *The Talented Mr. Ripley*. Fresh from his smashing success with *The English Patient* (1996), Minghella felt that Matt would be perfect as the sociopath-driven-to-murder.

According to Damon, to be pursued by two such powerful and popular directors is every actor's fantasy. "It's everything I've always dreamed of," he claims, "but it's an avalanche of offers—and I've never really thought about what

"I totally believe you should do things to better the world."

would happen if I actually got to this point. It's wonderful and daunting at the same time."

Actually, the film *Saving Private Ryan* had come along before *Good Will Hunting* was even released. It had begun filming on June 17, 1998, and was wrapped up by September 13, 1997.

"I'd auditioned by tape for *Saving Private Ryan*," Matt recalls, "but Steven thought I still looked like I did in *Courage Under Fire*. So when he actually saw me, he saw that I didn't look that way anymore, and that's what made the difference."

Having just worked for Steven Spielberg on *Saving Private Ryan*, and Francis Ford Coppola on *The Rainmaker*, he was doubly thrilled to have been employed recently by two of the most powerful and financially successful producer/directors in the film business. "[Steven Spielberg and Francis Ford Coppola are] both geniuses," he proclaims. "Francis indulges the actors a lot more, whereas, with Steven, it's about his movie. But Steven's very inclusive. He'll get the actors together and say, 'See, here's what we're gonna do. It's gonna be a really cool shot.' It's kinda like being in a group of kids who stole their father's camera and have to get it

With Ed Norton in *The Rounders*.

all in this one scene."

According to Coppola, "Actors like Matt are in as good a position as they've ever been. They've become the trademarks of the movies, not the directors. There's barely a movie that can be made without [Nicholas] Cage, or [Harrison] Ford, or [Brad] Pitt. Now they determine what movies get made. Matt has the gift—and he's a writer in his own right. That gives him something special."

Also in the works at the same time he received the Academy Awards nomination was his next film, *The Rounders*, co-starring Edward Norton, John Turturro, John Malkovitch, and Martin Laudau. When asked how the nominations affected his day-to-day life, Matt proclaimed from the New Jersey set of *The Rounders*, "I don't feel any different. I'm standing in a parking lot in Atlantic City. I still work 15 hours a day."

No sooner than he was finished with *Rounders*, than it was off to Europe to appear in director Anthony Minghella's *The Talented Mr. Ripley*. With location filming in Rome, Naples, and Venice, Italy, commencing in May of 1998, the talented Mr. Damon was off and running again. According to

Ed Norton and Matt Damon in New York City filming *The Rounders*, January 1998.

A scene from *Saving Private Ryan*.

Minghella, "There's something so apple pie about him. You know he was the best-looking kid in his school, won all the awards at track and field and dated the most popular girl."

Also on his list of forthcoming films is *Dogma*, in which he co-stars with Ben Affleck. The dynamic duo appears as a pair of angels attempting to get back to planet Earth. In the film, which is being directed by Kevin Smith of *Chasing Amy* fame, Emma Thompson portrays the role of God. The cast also includes Chris Rock and Alan Rickman. This will mark Matt and Ben's first screen performance together since *Good Will Hunting*.

In addition to all of these screen performances, Matt has already completed work on the animated film *Planet Ice*. Besides his work as the voice for the character of Cale, several other celebrities are putting their voices to the other cartoon characters. The all-star voice-over cast also includes Drew Barrymore, Bill Pullman, Nathan Lane, and Hank Azaria.

Ever since filming *Good Will Hunting*, Matt has literally been hopping from one movie set to the next. Now that he has all of this fame, he hasn't had a minute to really relax and enjoy it. "I don't have an apartment," he explained, "my stuff is in a warehouse in New Jersey. I'm making three movies in a row for all this money . . . I'm not complaining, you know, but I mean, why is it all happening to me? And if people are expecting this much, will they be mad if I let them down? I don't want to be a flash in the pan. I don't want to lose it all."

Matt is also determined not to allow his newfound fame to go to his head. With both feet planted firmly on the ground, he states, "Fame will f*** you if you're not ready for it, and it will f*** you if you're not grounded. I've got a great family, and I'm surrounded by people I love and trust who will not hesitate to knock me down if they see me getting arrogant."

While he and Leonardo DiCaprio are suddenly the hot movie-star sex symbols of the day, Matt is the first to discard any notion that he is the current "hunk" of the month. "I won't be Matthew McConaughey," he claims. "I'm not as good-looking as him. I'm certainly never going to be anyone's sex symbol."

His mother, Nancy Carlsson-

Paige, is downright disgusted at the notion that her son's artistic accomplishments are being used on magazine covers, when the magazine's sole purpose is for the readers to be confronted with ads for cigarettes, liquor, and other consumer goods. "I'm not happy about it particularly," she maintains. "What happens in a consumer society is that people become objects of attention in a way that doesn't seem healthy to society. I'm happy that Matt is happy in his work, but I'm not convinced he has to be on the cover of a magazine about it. It's a little hard for me to accept. It's all so out of the ordinary that I worry he might not grow as I want him to."

His mom is also not very happy about the fact that her son has yet to resume his last year in college. "I'm on a nine-year plan at Harvard. I was supposed to graduate in '92, and I did walk with my class at the commencement. My mother said, 'It's so consistent. There you were, pretending to graduate. It's what you've been doing your whole life.'"

Along the way to his new-found stardom, Matt Damon has had time to see up close and per-

Matt Damon in *The Rounders*.

sonally how the whole industry actually works—from the inside out. He especially isn't into getting wrapped up in self-destructive behavior, for either his personal life or his career. Marlon Brando and his whole excessive lifestyle clearly upsets him. "I think Marlon Brando has done more to destroy this generation of actors," Damon claims, "because, with the whole marble-mouth thing—the I-don't-give-a-f*** mentality—what people overlook is that when the dude was my age he was the hardest-working man in show business. He was onstage, he was busting his ass with [famed drama coach] Stella Adler, he was obsessed with acting. When people say, 'I just want to be fat and live in Fiji and have everyone tell me I'm a genius,' they're not looking at what it actually takes to get there."

He also doesn't think that he should get up on a soapbox and announce his politics, simply because he has a recognizable face at the moment. According to him, "Because somebody is on a television show or in a movie, does that qualify them to talk about an important issue? I have no problem with people who walk it like they talk it, but very few people do. It's easy when everybody's

paying attention to you to say, 'Well, here's a cause.' But very few actors are moving out of their houses and getting out of their Range Rovers to pick up their fellow man. Those few who do are the real thing, and they usually don't talk about it."

He also has some very definite ideas when it comes to lending his name or his presence to charity events. "I totally believe you should do things to better the world," he says, "but oftentimes there's so much bulls*** that just rings so hollow it kinda mucks up the waters. But then there's a well-known actor I know who has a life goal to change the laws so that tax credits will be given to big corporations for investing in orphanages. He's got a whole system worked out, but it's not about *him*. I think that some actors are more interested in having people think they want to help people than in actually helping them."

Throughout all of the success that Matt has had heaped upon him in the past year, the one aspect of his life that has not changed in any way, shape, or form, is his relationship with his best friend, Ben Affleck. According to Matt, "Ben's too modest to tell you this, but he's the most well-read person I know. He's certainly a lot smarter than I am."

The most critical thing that Ben can say about his buddy has to do with his housekeeping abilities. "Matt isn't the kind of person you can count on with dirty dishes, but when it comes to acting, he's the most focused, disciplined person I know," says Ben with a smile.

Says Matt: "Ben and I've lived together in probably ten different apartments with ten other people who we grew up with at different times, and the arguments are always the same. For example, I'm a slob and I get yelled at for not cleaning up when the house is a mess."

They also believe in total honesty in their friendship, and with regard to each other's personal relationships. Says Ben, "There's respect, but I think you have a false relationship if you pretend all the time that everything's fine. I think you can only have a healthy friendship with somebody if you're willing to say, 'Listen, man, you're not f***ing picking up after yourself,' or 'The person you're dating is obnoxious.' I think that happens and you kind of accept it."

One of the funniest things that Ben has said about Matt came on the *Oprah* TV show, when he proclaimed. "If I ever woke up with a dead hooker in my hotel room, Matt would be the first person I'd call."

What is the secret to maintaining a friendship such as theirs? According to Ben, it is quite a simple formula: "We're not competitive."

Now that they are both Academy Award winners, as far as ambitions go, what does Matt want to do with his stature in Hollywood? "Whenever someone offers, I'd love to direct with Ben Affleck. We've been friends since we were lads, and we don't let our egos get in the way of our work," he claims.

Matt and Ben are already plotting their next co-writing project. It is the screenplay to *Halfway House*, the compelling story of two substance-abuse counselors in Boston. As of early 1998, Matt explained, "It's sort of a low-concept stepchild of *Good Will Hunting* and about five [pages so far] are good."

Whether you think of him as a "hunk," a "sex symbol," or just a great fresh-faced young actor who has finally reached his stride, Damon is the hot Hollywood star to watch. Aside from his on-screen credentials, he is a bona-fide original who brilliantly proves that nice guys can finish first. Aside from his appealing and genuinely connected acting talent, he and his best buddy, Ben Affleck, together have a bright future ahead of them as screenplay writers as well. They have both worked hard, paid their dues, and are finally in a position to do some of their best and strongest work. More than just a handsome face on the screen, there is a truly exciting new face on the screen who is winning awards and capturing hearts along the way. He is chasing a dream, and his name is Matt Damon.

> Aside from his on-screen credentials, he is a bona-fide original, who brilliantly proves that nice guys can finish first.

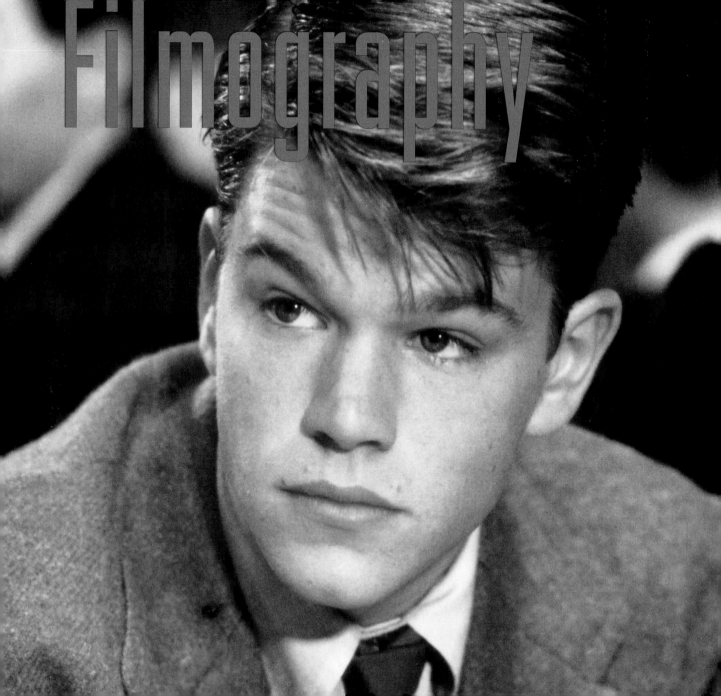

Mystic Pizza

October 21, 1988*

DIRECTOR:
Donald Petrie

CAST:
Julia Roberts
Annabeth Gish
Lili Taylor
Vincent D'Onofrio
William R. Moses
Adam Storke
Conchata Ferrell
Matt Damon

Rising Son

TNT Cable TV Movie;
July 23, 1990*

DIRECTOR:
John David Coles

CAST:
Brian Dennehy
Piper Laurie
Matt Damon
Jane Adams
Ving Rhames
Earl Hindman
Tate Donovan

School Ties

School Ties

September 18, 1992*

DIRECTOR:
Robert Mandel

CAST:
Brendan Fraser
Matt Damon

Chris O'Donnell
Randall Batinkoff
Andrew Lowery
Cole Hauser
Ben Affleck
Anthony Rapp
Amy Locane
Peter Donat

School Ties

Good Will Hunting

Geronimo: An American Legend

December 10, 1993*

DIRECTOR:
Walter Hill

CAST:
Jason Patric
Gene Hackman
Robert Duvall
Wes Studi
Matt Damon

Rodney A. Grant
Kevin Tighe

The Good Old Boys

TNT Cable TV Movie;
March 5, 1995*

DIRECTOR:
Tommy Lee Jones

CAST:
Tommy Lee Jones
Terry Kinney

Frances McDormand
Sissy Spacek
Sam Shepard
Wilford Brimley
Walter Olkewicz
Matt Damon
Blayne Weaver
Brucer McGill
Park Overall

Courage Under Fire

July 12, 1996*

DIRECTOR:
Edward Zwick

CAST:
Meg Ryan
Denzel Washington
Lou Diamond Phillips
Michael Moriarity
Matt Damon
Bronson Pinchot
Seth Gilliam

Glory Daze

September 27, 1996*

DIRECTOR:
Rich Wilkes

CAST:
Ben Affleck
Sam Rockwell

Megan Ward
French Stewart
Vien Hong
Vinnie DeRamus
Kristin Bauer
Alyssa Milano
John Rhys-Davies
Matt Damon

Chasing Amy

April 4, 1997*

DIRECTOR:
Kevin Smith

CAST:
Ben Affleck
Joey Lauren Adams

Jason Lee
Dwight Ewell
Jason Mewes
Casey Affleck
Brian O'Halloran
Kevin Smith
Scott Mosier

Courage Under Fire

With Theresa Wright in *The Rainmaker.*

Saving Private Ryan

July 24, 1998

DIRECTOR:
Steven Speilberg

CAST:
Tom Hanks
Tom Sizemore
Edward Burns
Matt Damon
Jeremy Davies
Adam Goldberg

Dogma

To Be Announced 1998/1999

DIRECTOR:
Kevin Smith

CAST:
Matt Damon
Ben Affleck
Emma Thompson
Alan Rickman
Linda Fiorentino
Chris Rock

The Talented Mr. Ripley

To Be Announced 1998/1999

DIRECTOR:
Anthony Minghella

The Rainmaker

November 21, 1997

DIRECTOR:
Edward Zwick

CAST:
Matt Damon
Danny DeVito
Jon Voight
Roy Scheider
Mickey Rourke
Theresa Wright
Mary Kay Place
Claire Danes
Randy Travis
Dean Stockwell
Red West
Danny Glover

Good Will Hunting

December 5, 1997*

DIRECTOR:
Gus Van Sant

CAST:
Matt Damon
Robin Williams
Minnie Driver
Ben Affleck
Stellan Skarsgård
John Mighton
Casey Affleck
Cole Hauser
Patrick O'Donnell
George Plimpton
Patrick O'Donnell

CAST:
Matt Damon
Gwyneth Paltrow
Jude Law
Cate Blanchett

Rounders

To Be Announced 1998/1999

DIRECTOR:
John Dahl

CAST:
Matt Damon

John Malkovich
Ed Norton
John Turturro
Martin Landau
Gretchen Mol
Melina Kanakaredes

Planet Ice

Animated; To Be Announced
1998/1999

DIRECTOR:
Art Vitello

VOICE-OVER CAST:
Matt Damon
Bill Pullman
Drew Barrymore
Nathan Lane
Hank Azaria
Lina Olin
Jim Breuer

* Available on Video

With Ben Affleck in *Good Will Hunting*.

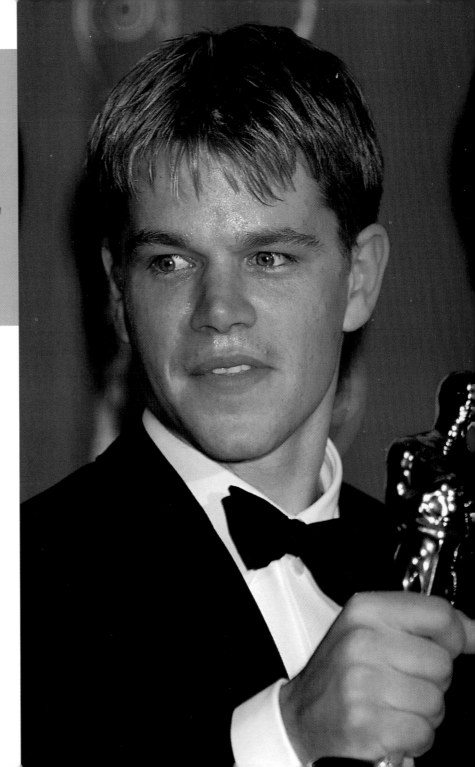

Matt's status in the business has gone from "so unknown he couldn't get arrested" to "unbelievably hot."